Welcome to Normandy

You can start exploring Normandy with this great book of games... A wonderful journey awaits you. With each page turned, you will learn heaps of fascinating and surprising new things.

Have fun on your adventure!

To make reading easier for you, difficult words have been highlighted in pink, and are explained in the glossary *p.59.*

Getting your bearings

Hello, my name is Camille and this is my younger sister, Jade. We were both born in Normandy.

This book of games will be perfect for exploring our region with you. We really love it here. Would you like to know why? Follow us!

Bois-des-Moustiers Park
35
Étretat
40
Neufchâtel-en-Bray
55
Le Havre
38
Arromanches-les-Bains
24
Jumièges
44
Rouen
16
12
Bayeux
Caen
9
34
Houlgate
48
Deauville
50
Honfleur
43
Bec-Hellouin
Lisieux
Évreux
57
Giverny
Clécy
52
Falaise
10
Norman Switzerland
55
Camembert
35
Pin-au-Haras
Carrouges
56
Nature park
Alençon
Nature park
Talked about in your book.

Let's speak French!

Would you like to discover the French language? Here are a few vocabulary words you can use to have fun learning French...your parents will definitely be impressed!

Oui/non
Yes/No

Au revoir
Good bye

Bonjour
Hello

S'il vous plaît
Please

À bientôt
See you soon

Parlez-vous anglais ?
Do you speak English ?

Merci
Thank you

1 un

2 deux

3 trois

4 quatre

5 cinq

6 six

7 sept

8 huit

9 neuf

10 dix

Cut along the dotted lines, tape both parts together and create a concertina fold.

Normandy's history in a nutshell

1469

End of Normandy's Duchy.
The region was attached to the kingdom of France.

1944

World War II began (1939-1945).
On 6 June, Allied soldiers landed on the beaches in Normandy and went on to France. (see p. 16)

1204

Normandy was integrated to the King of France's realm.

1337 - 1453

Hundred Years' War.
France and England were fighting.
Normandy went back to being English in 1418 then was conquered for good by the French in 1450.
France won the war.

Cut along the dotted lines, tape both parts together and create a concertina fold. →

1st century
after Jesus Christ

Gauls first settled down in the area 2,500 years ago. Like the Bretons, they fiercely resisted Julius Ceasar's army, but finally had to admit defeat.

9th century

The Vikings - men from Denmark and Norway - invaded the region. These tremendous warriors would pillage villages and abbeys and terrorise the population.

911

Rollon, the Viking chief, married the King of France's daughter (Charles III the Simple). Normandy was thus created. It became a Duchy and Rollon became the very first Duke of Normandy.

1066

William, Duke of Normandy, conquered England and became King. He was thus named "William the Conqueror". (see p. 10)

In Caen sights to see

You cannot talk about Caen without mentioning William the Conqueror. As the Duke of Normandy, this legendary hero placed the city at the very centre of his duchy. He quite naturally **decided to have his castle built here.** That was in 1060. Nowadays, the fortress is right in the heart of Caen. All its Middle Age ramparts are still standing. Its inside is now a lovely place to stroll around. They also came up with the great idea of opening the **Museum of Normandy** and **Museum of Fine Arts** there. Lastly, you can climb up onto the wall walk and enjoy the most beautiful panoramic view of the city. Get your swords ready!

Game

The Castle in Caen is one of the vastest medieval fortresses in Europe!

Calculate how long its ramparts are by following the example on the pyramid.

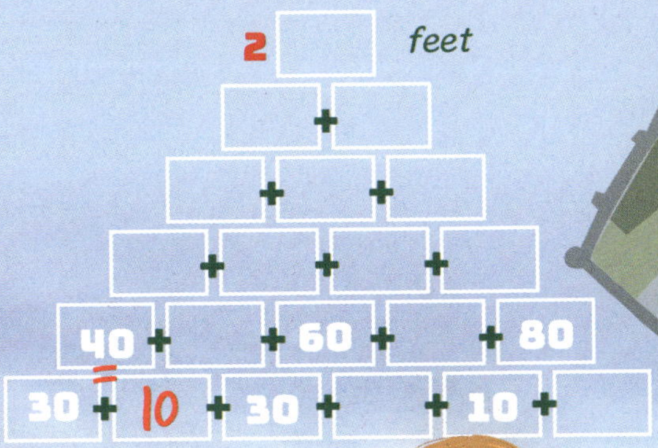

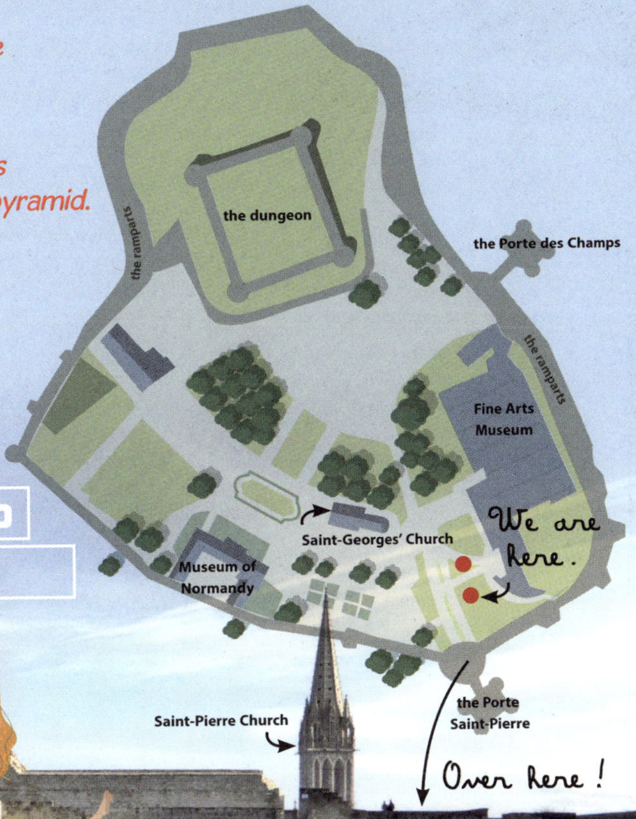

William the Conqueror (1027-1087)

statue of William The conqueror in the city of Falaise

Caen's Old Town

The other day, our grandfather showed us photos of our town before World War II. It is hard to imagine now, but in 1944 during the battle of Normandy, Caen was bombarded and 80% of it was destroyed!

Luckily, when strolling through the city, you will still come face to face with buildings that were spared, dating back to the Middle Ages. One of them is the **Quatrans House**, one of the few remaining with wood panelling *(see p.43)*. It was built towards the end of the 14th century.

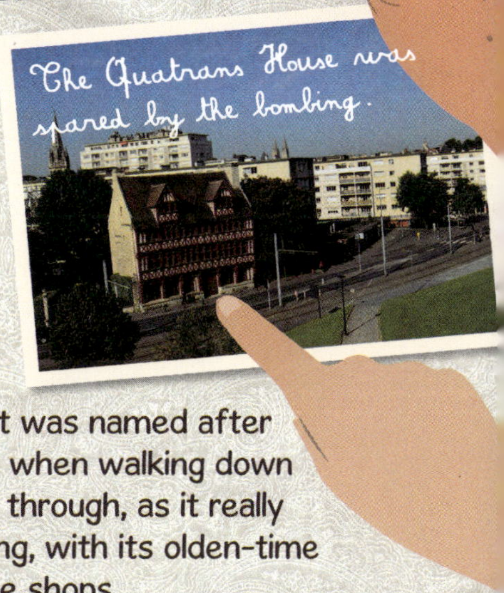

Nearby, you can wonder down one of Caen's oldest streets. For a long time, it was the printers' street. It was named after the chilly gusts of wind felt when walking down it. Its name does not suit it through, as it really is quite warm and welcoming, with its olden-time atmosphere and quaint little shops.

Game

Find the name of the street by placing the printers' block letters in the right order.

__ __   __ __ __

__ __ __ __ __ __

The first (very) large comic strip

Bayeux tapestry, 11th century - special authorisation from the City of Bayeux.

A famous discovery awaits you in the little town of Bayeux: **the tapestry of Queen Matilda***. It is also quite simply known as **the Bayeux tapestry**. Measuring close to 230 feet long, this huge embroidery woven on a linen canvas tells the story **of how William the Conqueror conquered England. That was in 1066.** Life in the Middle Ages seems to come alive before our very eyes all along this fresco. More than 600 characters, 200 horses and dozens of ships are depicted in it. A true comic strip dating back to the 11th century. Amazing.

** Matilda was William the Conqueror's wife and therefore the Duchess of Normandy and Queen of England.*

Let's now go over the scenario shown in this work.

William

King Edward

Harold

The year was 1064. In England, the old King Edward of England could feel his death approaching. Yet he had no children and therefore no successor. He thought that William, Duke of Normandy and a distant cousin of his, could take over the throne. **Edward therefore asked Harold, his brother-in-law, to go and tell William.**

Harold crossed the Channel and took an oath before William: he swore to support him after Edward's death. But Harold was somewhat deceitful. When Edward died on 5 January 1066, the funeral had barely ended before Harold took his place as Duke of Normandy and became King.

When William found out, he was furious and vowed not to let him get away with it. A few months later, he arrived in England with an impressive army behind him. Harold and his troupes were definitely in trouble.
On 14 October 1066, both armies fought near the village of Hastings - in the South of the country. The battle was fierce.

In the end, **Harold died after receiving an arrow in his right eye** and the Normans came out victorious. **William became King of England and is still today known as William the Conqueror.**

Game

Place the following dialogues in the right speech bubbles.

"AAAAh!"
"I swear to support you."
"Go to France now to warn my cousin!"
"Attack!"

You can also colour the pictures in.

Learning to WEAVE

The Bayeux tapestry was woven using **two very simple embroidery stitches.**

- **The stem stitch:** for all the outlines, lines on the faces, hands, legs and writing.
- **The couching stitch, also referred to as the Bayeux stitch,** which we have explained below. There are **three stages:**

❶ The stretch thread

To fill in the surface.

❷ The crossing thread

To keep the laid work in place. There is about 1/8 inch between each crossing thread.

❸ Picot stitch

To keep the crossing thread in place. Picot stitches are repeated every 1/8 inch.

What about colour?

The tapestry's woollen thread was dyed **using plant extracts.** Indeed, some plants have very powerful colouring agents. For example, red is obtained using **madder roots,** and blue is achieved using **woad.**

Onion peels are a home-made "dye" that you can easily try out at home. Test it first on an old piece of cloth.

Fill a saucepan with onion peels. Cover in water and boil <u>for 1 hour</u>.

Wet your cloth in clean water, then gently dip it into the hot dye.

Leave to set for <u>1 day</u>.

Rinse with cold water until it runs clear. You will get a beautiful golden colour!

Norman recipe

bourdelots or douillons?

with apples → bourdelots

with pears → douillons

What you will need:

SHORTCRUST PASTRY

- 200 g of flour
- 1 tablespoon of sugar
- 100 g of lightly salted butter
- 5 cl of water

FILLING

- 4 small orchard apples (Chantecler variety for example) or pears
- 4 tablespoons of sugar
- 1 egg yolk

And another 20 g of butter...

ADULT SUPERVISION REQUIRED

1 Prepare the pastry by mixing the flour, sugar and cut-up butter with your fingers, until you get a crumbly texture.

Gently add some water and roll into a ball.
Leave the pastry to sit for 30 minutes.

2 Wash the apples and remove the centre using an apple corer. You can peel them if you want.

Pre-heat your over to 160°C.

3 Mix 20 g of butter with the sugar and fill the middle of the apples.

4 Separate the pastry into 4 and roll each piece out big enough to wrap an apple inside. Close the pastry up on top.

Cut leaves in the remaining pastry and draw some veins. Stick them on top as decoration.

5 Cover the pastry in beaten egg yolk.

6 Cook for 45 minutes, the pastry should be golden-brown.

To be enjoyed warm!

6 June 1944: landings in Normandy

In 1944, the world was at war. It was World War II (1939-1945).
There was a clash between two major groups of countries:

- On the one side, **the Axis**: Germany, Italy and Japan.
- On the other side, **the Allies:** namely the United Kingdom, the United States, Canada and Russia.

Nazi Germany was the one who started the conflict. Its leader, **Adolf Hitler,** wanted revenge for his country, defeated during the previous war (1914-1918). In 1940, he succeeded in conquering France, which was then occupied by the German army. Because of this, in 1944, the Allies launched a huge attack to liberate France: **the D-day landings**. Code name: **operation Overlord.**

This attack was prepared by the Americans, English and Canadians in deepest secrecy. They started by making the Germans believe the landings would be further North in France, closest to the English coast. And it worked.

The Allies actually chose Normandy's coastline as it had so many advantages: vast beaches, easy access and protection from the Western winds.

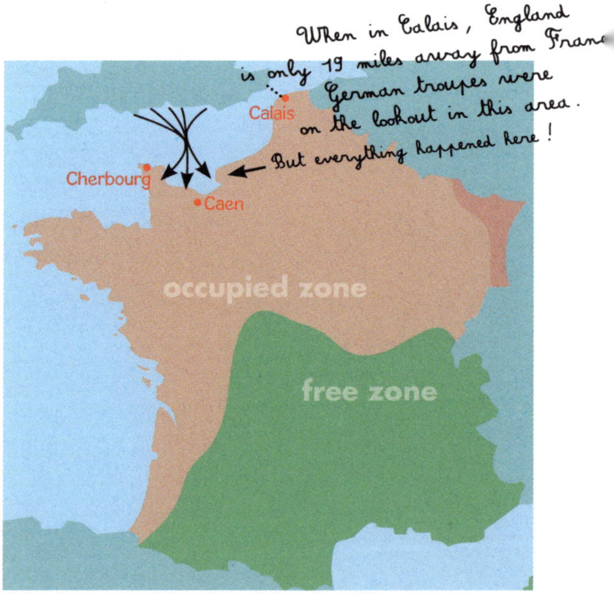

The day of the landings, also known as "D DAY", was only decided at the last minute: **it would be on 6 June.** That day, **140,000 Ally soldiers** arrived on **five beaches** in Normandy, that were later named: SWORD, JUNO, GOLD, OMAHA and UTAH. This was a decisive move.

Allied forces were then able to bring over more troupes and equipment to pursue their attack in France *(see next page).*

An American parachutist during the landings.

Arromanches,
an unlikely floating port

Once the troupes had landed, the allies needed to bring vehicles, more soldiers and additional food into France for the operation to be a success.
Problem: **Normandy's ports were all at the hands of the Germans.** And they could not be taken back.

At that stage, **Winston Churchill**, the English Prime Minister, had a crazy idea: **to build the port in several pieces**, in England, and tug it over the Channel to France. This led to the creation of the famous artificial port of Arromanches - a small town right near the landing beaches.

For months, thousands of English workers laboured day and night to complete this floating port.

In the afternoon of the 7th of June, **a convoy arrived in Arromanches.** The construction work could begin.

Operation name:

Mulberry B

Purpose:
To build a port in less than 15 days (it would normally take several years) so supplies could be provided to troupes after the D-day landings.

How:
By manufacturing the parts separately, like a huge Lego, and transporting them across the Channel.

Construction stages:

The first task was to set up dykes to outline the port and create a sort of large lake, protected from the waves and currents.

1 To do so, they sank **17 old ships** to form a first barrier.

2 **115 reinforced** but hollow concrete blocks, known as *Phoenix caissons*, were shipped over from England.

3 Once they had arrived, **they were sunk** to form a 5-mile semi-circle.

4 The **unloading docks** were then installed. 5 They were linked to the beach thanks to walkways affixed to concrete floats. The best **sea-roads ever!**

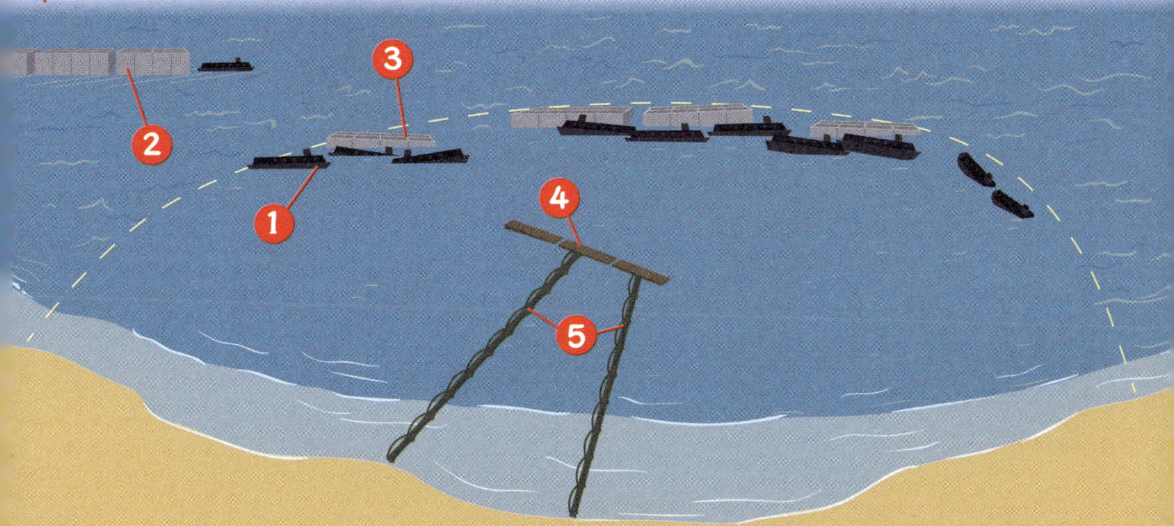

12 days after the D-day landings, the port was up and running. In total, it covered a surface area of **500 hectares** (700 football fields). Humongous!

At the expense of thousands of soldiers killed, **the Allies took over the coastline**, fought the Germans during a fierce battle in Normandy and **gradually liberated France**. Paris was liberated on 25 August 1944.

When visiting Arromanches, you can see the remains of this memorable adventure. Both out at sea and on the beach, **several concrete blocks and floaters can still be seen.**

To better understand this incredible operation, head to the **D-day Landing Museum**. There are lots of fascinating things to learn.

Granville

A rather original destination, with its upper and lower towns. On the one hand we have Uptown perched on its rock facing the sea. It was built in and around the ramparts, constructed in the 15th century. Under Louis XIV, the city walls were home to shipowners and privateers - formidable sea warriors.

In low town we have the beach, lined with a beautiful walkway. Up above us, an incredible villa looks down over the sea. Christian Dior (1905-1957), **the famous fashion designer**, spent his childhood there. The pink house and pink roses in the garden were actually a huge source of inspiration for him. The villa has now been turned into a museum, and visitors are filled with wonder before the creator's beautiful collections.

Game

Imagine what this dress' fabric could look like, drawing your inspiration from these pretty flowers.

Chausey Islands

The boats leave from Granville. After a 45-minute trip and a having crossed just over 10 miles, here we are in the Chausey archipelago. **An archipelago is a group of islands and islets**, and the Chausey one is the largest in Europe.

Chausey is almost like heaven on Earth. Around the main island, known as ***"Grande Île"*** (that only counts about fifteen inhabitants during the winter), the water is crystal clear, the sand is white and shore fishing is amazing. We almost forgot: when you come over to Chausey, you may be lucky enough to see dolphins or seals.

The Chausey archipelago's tidal range* can reach 377 feet.

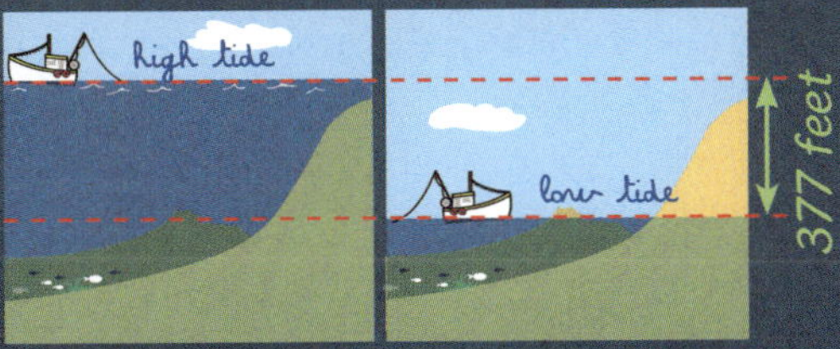

* The tidal range is the difference in water height measured between high tide and low tide levels.

Consequence: people say that the number of islets varies from 52 at **high tide** to 365 at **low tide**.

Using a blue felt-tip pen, have fun colouring over the small islets on this photo, as if it were high tide.

Chausey island archipelago - CNES photo library

Cherbourg-en-Cotentin

Cherbourg is the **city of ports**: commercial port, fishing port, passenger port (you can board a boat to England or Ireland from here), marina and military port (its dockyard is specialised in building submarines). The town can also boast about having the largest artificial roadstead in Europe!

If you come to Cherbourg, do not miss out on visiting the ***"Cité de la Mer"***. Set up in the former transatlantic **ferry terminal**, this incredible site will delve you into **a wonderful underwater world** (with its amazing 33-foot aquarium), allow you to relive the Titanic's last moments and take you on board the **"*Redoutable*" (meaning "the Impressive" in French) - the first French nuclear submarine built in 1967 in... Cherbourg.** Machines room, command post, torpedo **room**, welcome on board!

Game

Count the number of silhouettes for each item and finish the calculations to find out more about the Redoutable *submarine.*

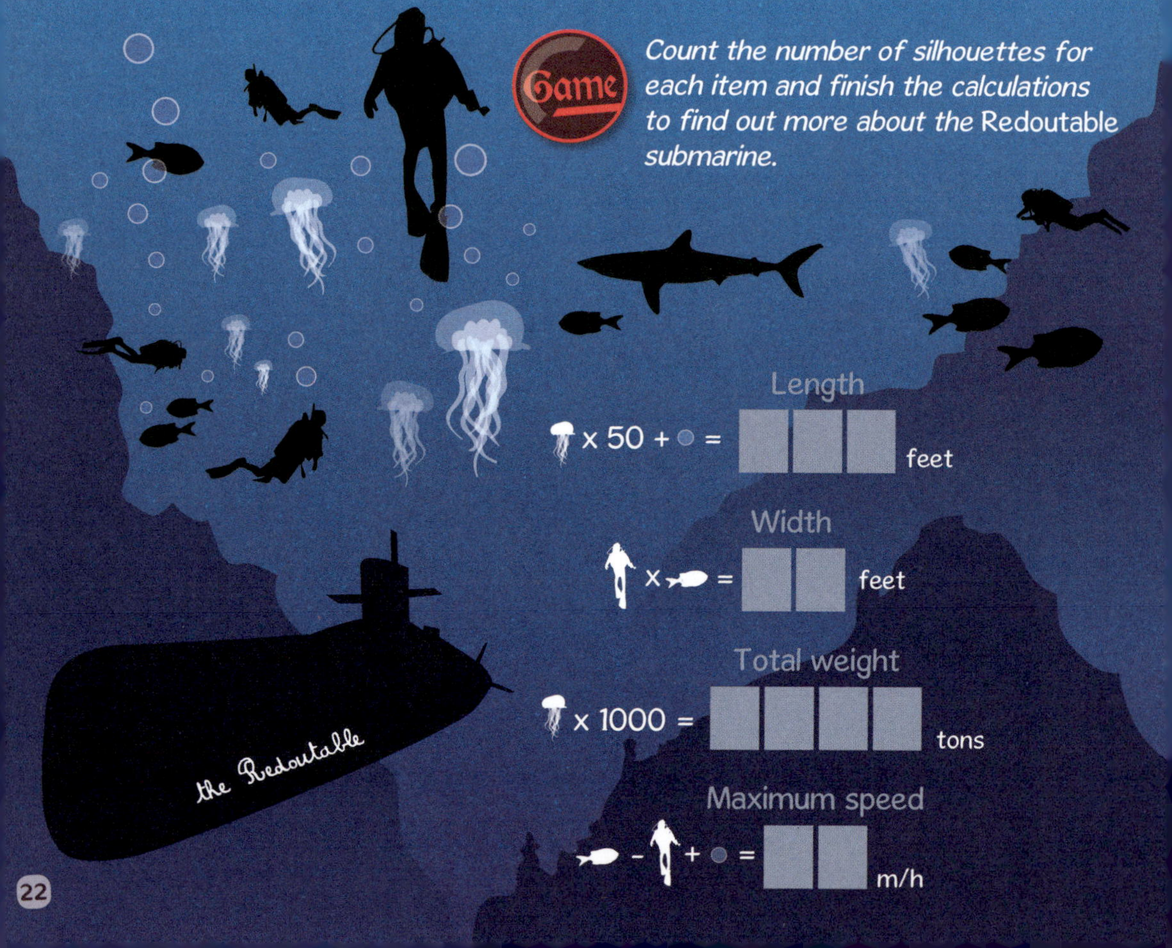

What a cast!

Welcome to Villedieu-les-Poêles, **welcome to the Cornille-Havard foundry.** They have been making bells here since 1865. More specifically, they cast them *(see game)*. Before, bell casters used to be non-sedentary and worked at the foot of the churches and cathedrals. Then, with the invention of railways, they had a new solution for transporting these heavy pieces weighing several tons.

Nowadays, there are only **two bell foundries left in France,** one of which is Cornille-Havard. The company can be proud of its history and **traditional know-how.** There is a reason why they were chosen to cast the most recent **bells in Notre-Dame cathedral in Paris,** installed in 2013.

In fact, this foundry can be visited. It would be a shame to miss out on it.

Game *Oh dear, Camille has mixed up the steps for making a bell. Can you help put them back in the right order, and add the right caption?*

1) They make the mould.
2) The metal is melted.
3) The metal is poured into the mould, which has been buried in a pit.
4) They leave it to cool for several days.
5) They remove the bell from the mould.
6) The bell is cleaned.
7) The bell is tuned.

Norman abbeys

Jumièges abbey in 1702 by Louis Boudan

Let's start by opening up our dictionaries:

Abbey: Large building where monks and nuns live. These people have chosen to live away from the rest of the world to pray and devote themselves to God. The church is right at the heart of the abbey.

There are more than forty abbeys in Normandy. That's a lot. Why are there so many? That question takes us back to the Middle Ages. To the 11th century, to be precise. Back then, Dukes had the power in the land *(see p.7)*. To celebrate their glory, and that of God, they built prestigious and sometimes even spectacular abbeys. To help them stand out, important aristocratic families soon began imitating them. A lot of new buildings were constructed.

*William the Conqueror had married Matilda, a distant cousin. This family tie was greatly frowned upon by the Pope. To redeem themselves, William and Matilda **each had their own abbey built in Caen.***

Game

Discover the name of these two abbeys by replacing each letter with the one that comes before it in the alphabet. (example: B=A)

NFO'T BCCFZ

_ _ _ ' _ _ _ _ _ _

XPNFO'T BCCFZ

_ _ _ _ _ ' _ _ _ _ _ _

A must-see: Jumièges abbey

It is nicknamed "the most beautiful ruin in France".

Though terribly damaged, its remains still enthral us all. As does its majestic open-sky church.

Places filled with literature and knowledge

In olden times, before printing was invented (towards 1450), books were **copied out by hand** by monks.
They were known as **copyist monks**. Settled down in a huge workshop within the abbey, called **the scriptorium**, they spent their days copying or translating manuscripts. They also decorated the texts for illustration: this was known as **illumination**.
For the texts to be even more pleasant to read, the monks used to create **dropped initials**: ornate capital letters written much bigger than the rest of the letters and positioned right at the beginning of the text.
As you can imagine, books could quickly become true works of art. Thankfully, lots of them were well-preserved. The **Scriptorial of Avranches**, a manuscript museum, is home to those originally made in the Mont-Saint-Michel abbey. We definitely recommend visiting it.

Finish the illumination of this dropped initial using your colouring pencils. You can also create lots of others!

ABCDEF
GHIJKL
MNOPQR
STUVWXYZ

A marvel to behold

Picture a **gigantic granite rock** surrounded by water. Right at the top, a beautiful abbey and its church stand proudly. Welcome to the Mont-Saint-Michel, a fantastic town that attracts millions of visitors every year.

Let's go and explore this **architectural feat.**

Once upon a time

It all started in about 708. As he was sleeping soundly one night, Bishop Aubert of Avranches had a vision of Saint Michael the archangel, commanding him to build a sanctuary. Whereabouts? On a tiny rocky island, previously called Mount Tomb. It became **the very first church in Mont-Saint-Michel.** There is no trace of it at all today.

Creation of the abbey

We are now in 966. Richard 1st, Duke of Normandy, wanted to assert his authority. He had countless castles built in the area, and decided to **found a major religious site at the Mont-Saint-Michel** to welcome Benedictine monks.

The legend of the skull

The monks living there made an incredible discovery: **a skull with a hole in it.** They were convinced it was Aubert's. Legend indeed has it that archangel Michael pierced the Bishop's skull with his finger so he would understand how important his request was and see it through to the end. This finding made **the Mount extremely famous** and pilgrims from all over Europe started flocking there to see it. **The site needed to be** expanded to welcome them.

Incredible constructions

In 1084, an enormous **church** was finished. It was as long as the Mount is high: 262 feet! It was a true feat, because it was rested on the tip of the rock. To ensure enough support, the builders had to construct large rooms **(crypts)** all around the Mount to fill in the slope. Then, in the early 13th century, construction of the Mount's **Marvel** began. This was the name given to the building to the North of the Mont-Saint-Michel's abbey: an architectural masterpiece that can still be visited nowadays.

Look way up at the top.
A copper statue of Michael shines right up at the top of the abbey's spire.
It is entirely covered in gold foil.

The Mont-Saint-Michel and its bay have been registered as a Unesco World Heritage site since 1979.

They saved the Mont-Saint-Michel

The Mont-Saint-Michel is a **huge rock surrounded by water.** Long ago, it was even a few miles away from the shoreline. In 1880, **a dyke-road was built** to welcome the many tourists and pilgrims. Later on, cars could even come and park at the foot of the Mount! **The problem** was that because of this dyke (amongst other things), the water from the tides could no longer circulate. So, over time, **the water stopped taking the sand and sludge out to sea.** The Mont-Saint-Michel was therefore at risk of being sanded in and ending up in the middle of the countryside. Thankfully, a solution was found.

In 2009, a dam was built on the Couesnon - the nearby river that flows into the sea. When activated, it would work like a flusher, evacuating all the sediments out to sea and therefore reducing silting (when there is too much sand). **In 2014,** the dyke-road was destroyed and replaced with a **walkway bridge. Advantage:** the water from both the Couesnon river and the sea can flow beneath it.

Nowadays, cars are parked **just over a mile away from** the site, and visitors can get a shuttle bus to the Mount. During very powerful tides, when the sea is high, **the Mont-Saint-Michel goes back to being an island.** Phew!

Game

What are these two herons saying to each other now that they have returned to the Mont-Saint-Michel?

A D E H K

M N O R S

T V W Y

Fauna

and flora in the bay

The bay around the Mont-Saint-Michel is home to an exceptional and protected fauna: marine birds and mammals, shoreline and estuary fish. Not forgetting **the sheep** that graze on a kind a grass soaked in sea water: the famous **salt marshes**.

The bay's rich flora is also perfectly adapted to the salty environment.

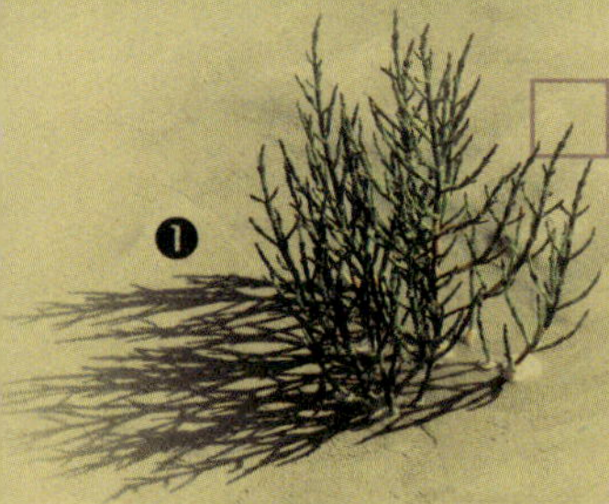

Game

Fill the grid with all the species living in the bay.

❶ GLASSWORT
❷ COMMON SHELDUCK
❸ BLACK-HEADED GULL
❹ HARBOUR SEAL
❺ SEA-BUCKTHORNE
❻ EEL
❼ BRENT GOOSE
❽ CUTTLEFISH

What a shell!

Scallops love living here on Normandy's coastline.
They enjoy the temperature of the water here, and the plankton is essential to their diet. As a result, 15 to 20,000 tons (2/3 of French fishing) of this bivalve mollusc are caught every year and sold at the ports of Dieppe, Fécamp and Port-en-Bessin-Huppain.
In 2002, Normandy's unrivalled scallops were awarded the ***"Label Rouge"*** quality certificate. This proves a product is of very high quality. Let's take a closer look at this special shellfish.

Game

An important piece of information is hidden amongst the scallop crates. Can you put the words in the right order?

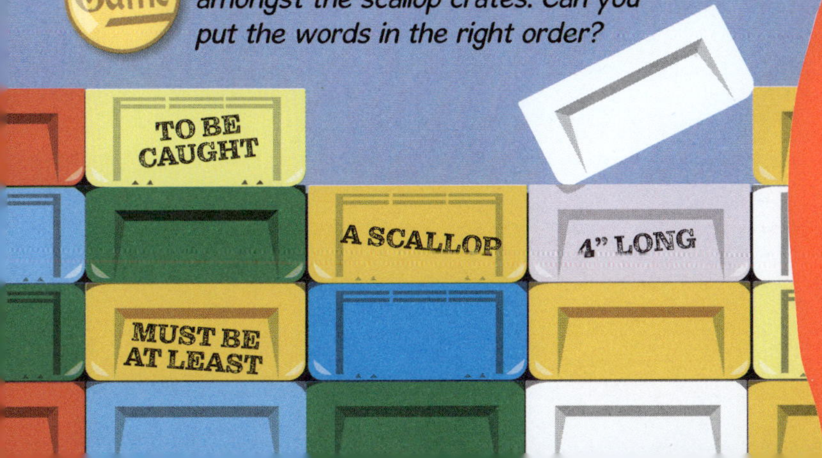

Shore fishing

We live according to the tides here on Normandy's coastline. And they can be particularly powerful over here. We call them **the Spring Tides**. When the sea withdraws, it leaves room for wide open stretches of sand and uncovered rocks. Paradise for shore fishing. You can gather an incredible amount of seafood. So, what's on the menu for tonight?

Game

In this grid, find all the shellfish and molluscs you can fish along the shore.

As you can see in the example, words can appear in any way possible, but WATCH OUT, each letter can only be used once.

SAND SHRIMP
VELVET CRAB
LOBSTER
CRAB
OYSTER
MUSSEL
WHELK
~~WINKLE~~
DOG COCKLE
COCKLE
CLAM
LIMPET

M	C	E	L	S	A	C	K	L
U	O	C	K	R	N	O		E
S	S	E	L	E	D	C	D	
L	O	Y	S	T	S	G	O	B
O	M	T	C	R	H	E	L	A
B	A	E	W	A	R	P	K	R
S	L	V	H	B	I	M	N	C
T	C	L	E	L	K	W	I	T
E	R	E	V	L	I	M	P	E

Fishing equipment:

→ a bucket,
→ a net for catching shrimp,
→ a ruler for measuring your shellfish*.

* More information can be found on the Internet.

To become the perfect fisherman:

→ Make sure to limit yourself to what you can eat that day!
→ Remember to measure your gatherings as you go along.
→ Remember to put any rocks you turn over back where you found them and the same way up, to preserve the ecosystem.

Spring tides

We know a lot about Spring tides here. Normandy has some of the biggest in Europe. We prepared a short presentation for you.

What is a tide?

Every day, the sea rises and goes down. This movement is called a tide. It happens 4 times a day, every 6 hours. There are two high tides and two low tides per day.

Why does the sea level go up and down?

1- Because the rain makes sea levels rise.

2- Because someone switched off the tap.

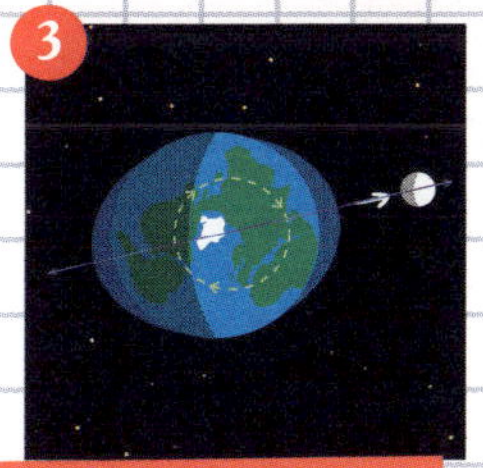

3- Because of the Moon's attraction.

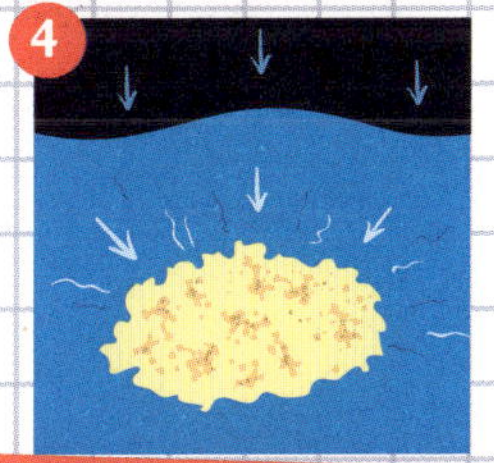

4- Because the sponges soak up all the water in the oceans.

3/ The Sun and most importantly the Moon have a pulling force on the sea. A little like a magnet, they attract the water's surface. Depending on their position, they make the sea level rise or drop.

What about the spring tides?

When the Earth, Sun and Moon align, the Sun's pulling force reinforces that of the Moon - making the tides much more powerful.

They are the strongest in March and September, during the spring and autumn equinox.

The huge American cemetery in Colleville-sur-Mer.
How moving !

The "Non-violence" sculpture in front of the Memorial in Caen.
A beautiful symbol.

Flat oysters
They are my favourite !

Notre-Dame de Bernay abbey
Right near our grandparents' house.

We all have our favourite spots and best memories.
Jade's are on the right-hand page.
And mine are here.

Going body boarding in front of the villas in Houlgate.

The umbrellas of Cherbourg

The most beautiful and robust umbrellas.
It is also the title of a film I like.

The show jumping competitions at the Haras du Pin centre.

Amazing!

"Confiture de lait" caramel spread.

A speciality! (Especially the one I make with mum.)

The flowers in the Bois-des-Moutiers park.

My favourites? The tulips... they are almost black!

Smelling the lovely scent of heather running along the Ecalgrain bay on the path in the Cotentin area.

Paradise for impressionists

In the second half of the 19th century, a new pictorial movement began in France: impressionism. **Rather than representing precise reality, impressionists preferred to paint their impressions, feelings and moods.** They expressed themselves using small touches of colour. Shapes became less precise and shook up habits. At first, these painters actually received a lot of criticism.

Game

Spot the 7 differences between these two impressionist paintings.

Impressionists also loved to work **outdoors, with a lovely landscape before them.**

With the sea nearby and its ever-changing light, Normandy became a true open-sky workshop for this form of art. From Rouen to Dieppe, stopping off in Étretat, the most famous artists came to rest their easel in this region: **Renoir, Courbet, Pissaro** or even **Eugène Boudin,** considered as one of the very first impressionist painters. In fact, he influenced the most renowned amongst them: **Claude Monet** *(see p. 57)*.

A painter's best friend

At the same time, a major invention changed painters' lives: **metal tubes of paint**. Before, colours used to be prepared by hand, using oil and coloured powders. It was time-consuming and cumbersome.
Tubes made everything so much more practical. Painters could leave **their workshops** and **paint in the great outdoors**.

Game

5 labels have come unstuck. Replace each colour on its tube, following the instructions below.

The tube of yellow is just next to one of the tubes of blue.

The 2 green tubes are far away from each other,

but the 2 blue tubes are side by side.

The red one is in between 2 tubes of orange.

The remaining tube is the black one.

Le Havre and Perret's architecture

On 5 September 1944, during World War II, ally bombings destroyed 80% of Le Havre's city centre. 50,000 people found themselves homeless. The city had to rebuild its housing quickly but properly. To do so, it decided to call upon a famous Parisian architect: **Auguste Perret** *(photo)*.

What made him stand out?
He was one of the first to rely on a new construction material: reinforced concrete. He then imagined an entirely modern town with an orthogonal design, leaving lots of room for wide open streets. Straight lines only! Lastly, the buildings were not made too high, to let lots of light through. Once finished, Le Havre became a city open onto the sky and nearby sea.

Game

Which construction is symmetrical to this set of buildings?

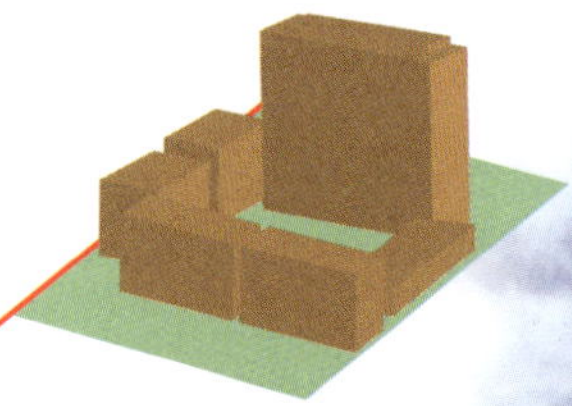

1

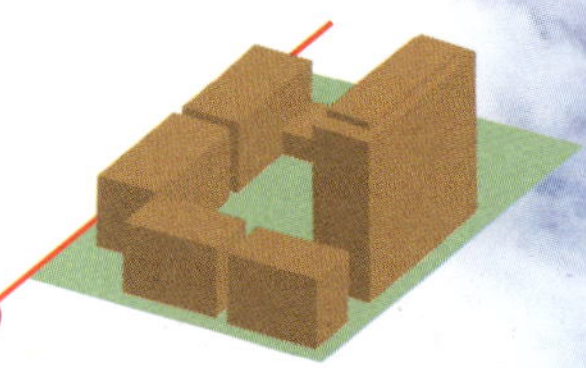

2

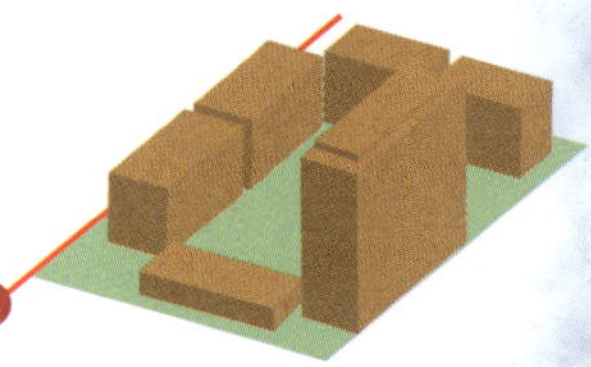

3

With all that concrete, Le Havre can sometimes be perceived as a little gloomy and grey. Despite this, since 2005 its city centre has been registered as a Unesco World Heritage site, based on this ingenious architecture. That is what you call true recognition.

Way up high!

A skyscraper? No, a church tower.
And what a church! Towering 351 feet high, you definitely cannot miss this lovely steeple. **It has become a landmark for Le Havre's tourists and citizens.** Like a lighthouse right in the middle of the city. When the weather is good, it can be seen from 37 miles away. This modern church is named Saint-Joseph and was built in 1951 by... **Auguste Perret.**

This architect definitely did not lack in imagination. The material used for its construction? Concrete. However, the most impressive part is inside. The bell tower *(photo)* lets the light in through its 12,768 stained-glass windows. The colours were chosen according to their orientation (East, West, South or North) and therefore change with the sun. How beautiful!

Game

Use the grid to help draw the other half of Saint-Joseph's church.

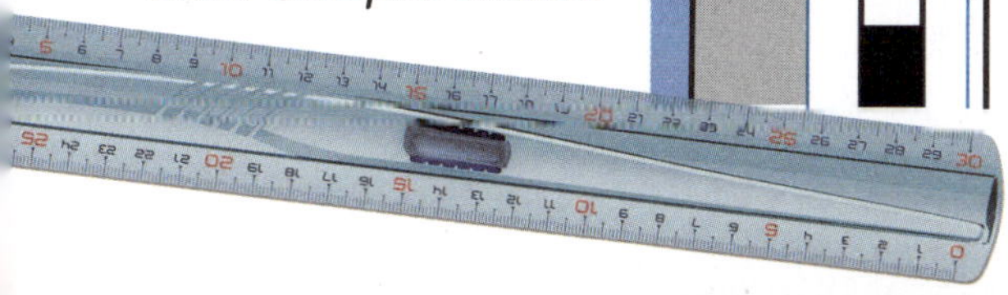

Get your ruler out so your lines are perfectly straight.

Étretat,
a natural marvel

Would you fancy walking **by the sea, 330 feet high?** In Étretat, it's possible. People here walk along the white limestone cliffs, that drop vertically into the sea. Dizzying!
When Normandy's changing light falls onto the cliffs, it is quite simple breath-taking.

Who do we have to thank for this? Nature. 90 million years ago, it created this beautiful site. This is what we call erosion. It did such as great job that with some help from the wind, waves and an underground river, it dug **a natural arch plunging deep into the sea, and formed a 167-foot high needle.**

Going to Étretat is an unforgettable experience.

Étretat is a nice place to stop off along the 81 mile-long coast, where cliff after cliff look over pebble beaches.

Game *Discover* ***the name of this coastline*** *by filling in the grid using the colours in the list.*

CARROT	PISTACHIO
CHARCOAL	RUBY
EGGSHELL	SALMON
MINT	VIOLET
NAVY	

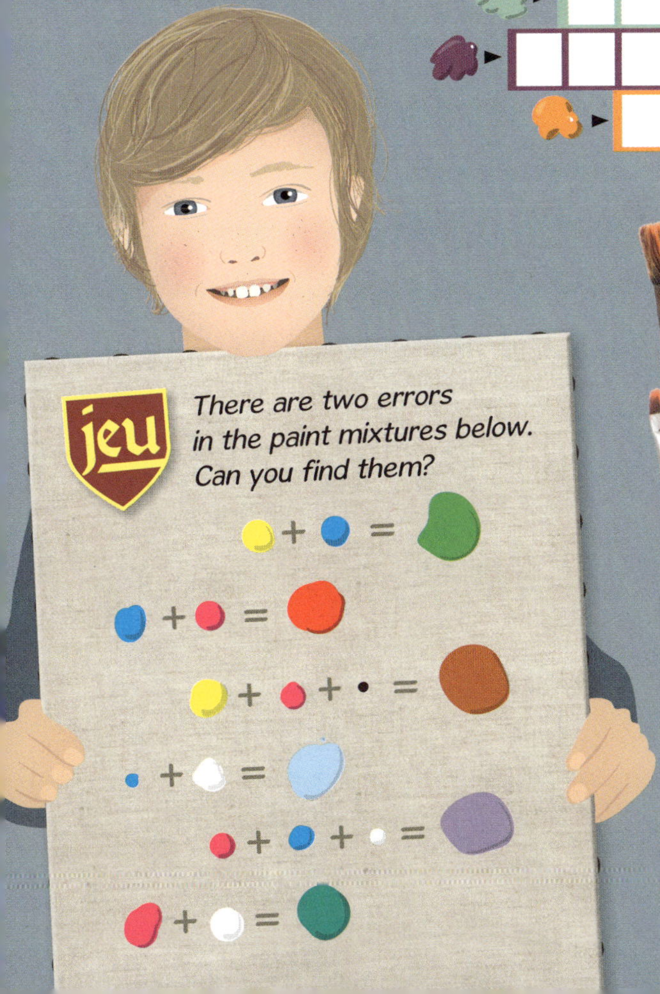

jeu

There are two errors in the paint mixtures below. Can you find them?

This spectacular backdrop drew in lots of **impressionist painters** *(see p. 36)*. Claude Monet devoted about fifty canvases to Étretat, and Gustave Courbet painted *Étretat's cliff after a storm*.

The Mystery of the Hollow Needle

The Hollow Needle is a crime novel by **Maurice Leblanc** (1864-1941), a French author who had a holiday home in Étretat. He wrote several of his books there.

This novel tells the story of **Arsène Lupin,** a "gentleman thief". He was nicknamed like that as he was such an elegant and flirtatious thief, who would steal from his victims without resorting to violence. This almost made him a nice person.

In this adventure, Maurice Leblanc tells us that Étretat's Needle is hollow and hides away a treasure. And guess who found out about that secret? Arsène Lupin, of course!

To resolve the real riddle on your own, head to the **Clos Lupin**, Maurice Leblanc's former house now open for visits. Go on an original journey to solve the mystery...

Game

Can you solve this first riddle?

The Needle's treasure belongs to the

- 1st letter of the 3rd paragraph (on the left).
- Last letter of the last name of the author.
- 3rd letter of "Mystery".
- 1st letter of Arsène Lupin's nickname.
- Last letter of Arsène Lupin's nickname.
- Twice in "book".
- Appears in "Arsène" and "Lupin".
- 11th letter of the alphabet.
- In the middle of "Maurice".
- Three times in "Needle".
- 1st letter of "Arsène".

Le Bec-Hellouin

Game

A few errors have slid into these photo bubbles. Only one of them is perfectly correct, which one?

No doubt about it, this little village gives us a taste of what Normandy truly is. As perfect as a postcard.
Surrounded by greenery and apple orchards, Le Bec-Hellouin is home to **a beautiful abbey** *(see p.24)* founded in 1034: **Notre-Dame-du-Bec.**

The village is tiny, but strolling through its flowery streets and past its colourful wood-clad houses makes for a very pleasant outing. These houses were very common in the Middle Ages, and are also known as **half-timbered houses.**

What are they? *Well, these little buildings stay standing thanks to wooden posts or beams (timber framing). To make the walls, the empty spaces between the beams were filled with light materials such as plaster or cob (mixture of earth and straw).* Such a pretty result!

Go back in time in Rouen

Your trip to Rouen will take you on a **fantastic journey through the Middle Ages**. Look at all these wood-clad houses *(see p. 43)*. You will spot them all over town. So charming.

If we had to choose a picture to represent Rouen as we know it, it would be "*Le Gros-Horloge*" (the Big Clock).

Indeed, the Gros-Horloge has a belfry (a tall tower) and a pavilion in which two beautiful dials were installed: one on each side.

The belfry

It dates back to the 14ᵉ century. It is home to two bells that have always rung on the hour and again every quarter of an hour. It was built using one of the oldest clock-making mechanisms in Europe. This mechanism makes the hands move around the dials and activates the bell-ringing.

The dials

They were first installed during the 16th century. Right in the centre lies a sun with 24 rays. Each dial only has **one hand, to tell the hour!** Don't worry, the one for the minutes was not broken. But at the time, people did not much care about the minutes. They settled for knowing what hour it was.

In the 16th century, only very few people could read it. So every day is represented by an ancient Roman god.

Game *Find which day goes with which god.*

And there is more. Right at the top of the dials is a ball, half black and half silver, that details **what phase the Moon is in**. For example, when it is completely silver, it is full moon.

The *Gros-Horloge* is decorated with lots of little sheep. Most of them were placed at the tips of the dials' hands. **The sheep is the symbol of Rouen.** In the Middle Ages, the town was indeed renowned for its sheep-wool sheets.

The *Gros-Horloge* can be visited. It is fascinating and definitely a must-see to understand the history behind it. At the top of the belfry, you can even enjoy a fantastic panoramic view of the city.

Joan of Arc

On 30 May 1431, Joan of Arc, **aged 19 at the time, was burned alive on the Old Market Square in Rouen** (the square still exists nowadays). Her ashes were thrown into the Seine - the river that crosses the city. But who was this young woman now considered a **national hero**?

1. We are in 1429, **and the Hundred Years' War had broken out**. The French were fighting against the English, who had invaded the Kingdom of France.
2. In the Lorraine area of France, in a pretty little village called Domrémy, **a young shepherdess named Joan of Arc** said she could hear mysterious voices asking her to liberate her country.
3. She travelled to meet the **King of France Charles VII** and persuaded him to **entrust her with a small army**. Joan of Arc pushed the English forces back in Orléans and liberated the city. A real feat!
4. She carried on fighting, but was unfortunately captured and handed over to the English in 1430. She was declared heretic, considered as a witch, and was therefore burned at the stake after a **memorable hearing**.

In the very heart of Rouen, exactly where the hearing took place, lies the **Joan of Arc historical museum** presenting a very instructive journey through our hero's epic adventures.

Game *Number these pictures drawn from Joan of Arc's life, putting them in the right order. Use the words in bold to help you.*

The **highest** cathedral in France...

It is **495 feet high** and located in Rouen.
People say its beautiful facade is made of **stone lace**.
Started in the 12th century, **Notre-Dame de Rouen** was further embellished until the 16th century.
It boasts a Gothic style.

The cathedral's choir is home to the recumbent statues of two Dukes of Normandy: **Rollon** (the Viking chief) and **Richard the Lionheart**.

Claude Monet painted the cathedral **28 times**, with varying lighting, at all times of the day, and during all the seasons.

Game One of the cathedral's towers was named after a typically Norman product. Find out what it is in this maze... watch out for the dead ends!

IT IS THE ______________ TOWER

During lent, this food used to be forbidden. Christians who wanted to eat some had to pay. In the end, it was thanks to them that the tower could be built.

Deauville
Along the wooden planks

Tourists from all over the world love coming to Deauville. This chic and stylish seaside resort definitely has a lot of advantages: luxury hotels, a casino and a white sandy beach over a mile long with colourful parasols all along it.

Yet what made the town so popular was actually its Planks. Its planks? Yes, that is what we call the wooden walkway that runs along the beach. Build in 1923, they were designed so elegant ladies could walk without dirtying their dresses. And they have been a real success ever since!

On the big screen

And the winner is...

Since 1975, every year in September, the biggest stars walk down the red carpet in Deauville for the town's **American Film Festival.** For 10 whole days, movie-lovers can watch about a hundred films (Hollywood productions , independent films, tributes, etc.). Prizes are awarded to the best of them.

Obviously, **this is the perfect time for meeting your favourite cinema stars.** Otherwise, you can head to the Planks to meet the legends that came to Deauville for its festival since its inauguration in 1975. **Their names are written on the small barriers** (we call them the "palisades") separating the beach huts. Walk along with the stars, and discover names such as: **Elizabeth Taylor, Clint Eastwood, Cate Blanchett, Matt Damon, Tom Hanks, etc.**

Honfleur

They say it is one of the most beautiful little harbours in Normandy. I would say in the whole of France. And that is not just became I'm from here. What makes it so charming? The Old Harbour, otherwise known as the port. It was created under the reign of Louis XIV. It is lined with slate-roofed houses, all squeezed against each other. They are very quaint and we can see their reflection in the harbour's water below. They definitely deserve everyone coming to see them!

Game

5 errors have slid into these pretty reflections. Keep your eyes peeled!

A few other curious sites await you in Honfleur. Starting with Saint Catherine's church. **It is the largest wooden church in France.** Constructed during the 15th century, it replaced an old stone church that was destroyed during the Hundred Years' War. They did not have many resources available, so the villagers used wood from a nearby forest. Well done! **The steeple also stands out: it is separate from the rest of the church.** Indeed, those who built it considered that the wooden roof would not be strong enough to bare the weight of the bells.

The separate steeple at Saint-Catherine's church

Not far from the church lies **the Eugène Boudin museum**. This renowned painter was born in Honfleur and is now considered as one of the pioneers of the impressionist movement *(see p. 36)*.
He was particularly good at painting infinite varieties of clouds. So much so that he was nicknamed **"the King of the skies"**. The museum is home to 105 of his works.

Eugène Boudin, *Portrieux Shoreline*, 1874

Draw some pretty grey and pink clouds to emphasize the evening light. You could also add a few touches of light using some chalk, or blur the lines a bit with your fingers.

Norman Switzerland

Oh, it's so lovely here. Of course it is, we have finally reached Norman Switzerland. What is that country doing all the way over here?

It gave its name to this area of Normandy because of its uneven, green and wooded terrain. It reminds us a lot of Switzerland's landscapes. Here, along the Orne river, Normandy rises above its plains. The highest peaks reach an impressive... 984 feet. We are obviously not in the Alps, but in certain places the landscapes are quite simply breath-taking. In any case, Norman Switzerland is true paradise for fishermen and sport-enthusiasts. Spend your free time hiking, mountain-biking, kayaking & canoeing, paragliding and rock-climbing.

Game

Can you help the sports club leader check that everyone has the equipment they need for the outing?

Each person needs:

1 life-jacket, 1 helmet, 1 paddle

What's missing?

........life-jacket(s), ...helmet(s), ...paddle(s)

The Rock of Oëtre, an incredible display of nature

Watch out, thrilling sensations up ahead! The Rock of Oëtre is a spectacular site set in the heart of Norman Switzerland. You will need to walk along a small path to get there. At the end of it lies a natural belvedere offering the most amazing panoramic view. The path actually leads to the edge of a chasm towering 387 feet high. And right there in front of you, if you look closely, you will see an incredible geological phenomenon. A rock in the shape of a human profile. Can you see it on this photo?

Game

Discover the name of the mountain stream running at the bottom of the chasm by linking the right letters with each bird.

Cows everywhere!

They are without a doubt our star animal here. Indeed, Normandy cows (you can also say "*La Normande*" to impress people) played a huge role in our region's reputation. They have their own special look: an attractive **coat** *(see game)* that is white with ginger or brown spots of various sizes. They also wear "glasses": they have dark circles around their eyes. Normandy cows can weigh a fair amount - up to 800 kg. Not bad, right?

Here in Normandy, they love grazing in the pastureland. When well fed, they produce extremely high-quality milk - rich in protein and fat. And guess what we make with this milk... We make cheese (Camembert, obviously), cream and butter (typically from Isigny). And it tastes amazingly good.

Game

*Normandy cows have three different **coats**. The names of these coats change according to their dominating colour.*

Discover the three coat names using the code.

dominance of white,
the coat is called:

dominance of light brown,
the coat is called:

dominance of dark brown,
the coat is called:

The country of cheese

As you now know, our very generous cows help us made lots of delicious types of cheeses. Among them, **four have a PDO label** (Protected Designation of Origin). This is a rare label that guarantees a product's origin and quality. Let's go and discover these four star pupils.

Each of these cheeses was named after its home village. Can you recognise them?

Neufchâtel

This is the oldest cheese in Normandy. It was mentioned as early as 1035. Legend has it that young girls from the area of Bray would give this heart-shaped cheese as a gift to English soldiers during the Hundred Years' War. Of course, we cannot be certain of that.

☐

Camembert

This one is pretty much our hero. Its name is known all over the world, and foreigners automatically think of France when they see it. It was first made in 1791 just a stone's throw away from the small village of Camembert, which now has its own museum. We definitely recommend a visit (and a tasting).

☐

Livarot

It is nicknamed "the Colonel" because once made it is wrapped in a strip of natural reed that goes five times around the cheese, like the five stripes of a colonel's grade. Initially, it used to prevent the cheese from collapsing during the maturing process.

☐

Pont-l'Evêque

With its rind ranging from yellow to orange, its fairly strong smell (the stables are nearby) and its square shape, this cheese knows how to stand out from the crowd. Its taste is however not as strong as its smell.

☐

Carrouges

Carrouges castellum

This castle has a great look to it. To get there, you need to enter through an impressive gateadorned with four circular turrets. That is what we call a castellum. What makes Carrouges castle stand out from the rest? **It was built using bricks.** Although some granite was also used. This is where its pretty pink hues come from. Construction began during the 14th century, and the castle was home to three families: the Carrouges, Blosset and Le Veneur families. The latter stayed until 1936. **With its plush period furniture** and countless family portraits, it almost makes us feel like someone still lives there. The tour finishes with **the monumental main stairway made of exposed pinky-orange bricks.** A true wonder.

Game

Place the right label on the correct piece of furniture.

Monet in Giverny

Without the shadow of a doubt, Claude Monet is still the most admired impressionist painter of them all *(see p. 36)*.

The reason for his success? The way he painted light. And more specifically the changes in light within a same landscape, depending on the time of day and weather.

He loved the great outdoors, lovely gardens and flowers, and would therefore **convey his impressions** when looking at nature. So, in 1883, to make the very most of nature and fulfil his passion for painting, he settled down in the small village of **Giverny. He created his own painting area there**. He built a large workshop and created a beautiful garden with a lovely oriental atmosphere.

His garden gave him the inspiration for 250 canvases*! They all depict a pond with water lilies, but none of them are the same.

Game *Discover the name of this series of paintings hidden away in the lake.*

Nowadays, if you go to Giverny, you can visit Claude Monet's house and discover he famous water garden. When strolling through it, it feels like you are walking in the artist's paintings. Wonderful!

**These world-renowned works of art can be seen at the Orangerie Museum in Paris, or at the André Malraux modern art museum in Le Havre.*

A Kingdom of apples

Here is another of our region's star products: the apple. There are more than 400 varieties here in Normandy. Not easy to remember all their names. So we will be showing you two of the most famous.

First of all, **the Benedictin.** People say it is the most delicious. **It owes its name to the Benedictine monks at Jumièges abbey.**

Next comes **the Jonagold.** It is very sweet, not too sour and has lovely orangey-red skin. Children generally love it.

REMINDER:
we use fermented apple juice to make cider - a delicious sparkling drink. The one from Normandy has a very good reputation. But watch out, it contains alcohol!

Game

Will this market gardener manage to fill all her apple crates if each one contains 20 apples?

Glossary of complicated words

Archangel Angel of a higher rank.

Aristocratic Aristocratic families belong to a higher class – they may be nobility for example.

Belvedere Large terrace built very high up, making for a great lookout point.

Bivalve (mollusc) A mollusc is a soft-bodied animal that lives in the water. It is considered to be bivalve when protected by a shell made up of two articulated valves. Mussels and oysters are examples of bivalve molluscs.

Dockyard The place where war ships are built and maintained.

Dyke Construction used to retain sea or river water.

Equinox Time of the year when the day and night last the same number of hours (spring and autumn).

Erosion When the land is worn down by the wind or sea.

Fermented That has undergone fermentation. Fermentation is the process via which sugar turns into alcohol through lack of oxygen and thanks to germs.

Gothic style Widespread architectural style in Europe between the 12th and 16th centuries, mostly used when building cathedrals. It stands out with its pretty vaults and large windows letting in lots of light.

Heretic Goes against the Church's beliefs.

Hollywood productions Huge and very expensive films produced by film studios located in Hollywood – in the town of Los Angeles in the United States.

Independent (film) A film produced without much money and outside major production studios.

Lent In the Christian religion, lent is a period of fasting that lasts from Ash Wednesday to Easter.

Maturing The last manufacturing stage when making cheese, when it becomes riper and develops all its flavours.

Nazi Supporter of Nazism, a movement directed by Hitler, that spread racist and warlike ideas (namely against Jews) during World War II.

Non-sedentary Travels around.

Occupied During World War II, France was occupied by the German army from 1940 to 1944. It was invaded and placed under Germany's domination.

Oriental From the Orient The Orient includes all the countries in Asia – to the East of Europe.

Orthogonal That forms a right angle.

Pastureland Land covered in grass (field, meadow) where animals come to graze.

Pictorial movement Artistic painting style that stands out from the rest.

Pilgrimage A journey made by a believer to a place that is sacred in their religion, such as Mecca for Muslims and Rome for Christians.

Pioneer Person who is the first to bring a new style or movement to the table, thanks to their ideas or inventions.

Plankton Microscopic animals and plants that live in the sea.

Recumbent statue A recumbent statue is a sculpture of a decease person lying down. It is usually placed on top of their tomb.

Reinforced concrete Concrete is a highly-resistant construction material made of cement, sand, gravel and water. In reinforced concrete, steel rods are added.

Roadstead Large surface of water opening out onto the sea where boats can moor.

Sanctuary A sacred place.

Sediments Natural deposit left by the water or wind.

Stripe Small ribbon sown onto a soldier's uniform, showing their grade.

Torpedo A weapon of war launched from a submarine.

Transatlantic Crossing the Atlantic Ocean.

Unesco World Heritage site To raise awareness about and preserve very important cultural and natural sites, the Unesco (United Nations Educational, Scientific and Cultural Organization) drew up a list that now counts over 1,000 sites throughout the world. For instance, Stonehenge in England and the Grand Canyon are registered on that list.

Wall walk A path right on top of the ramparts where people could walk to check what was happening on the outside.

Maturing of Camembert in Normandy

Answers

Page 9:

2 800 feet

380 | 420

180 | 200 | 220

80 | 100 | 100 | 120

40 | 40 | 60 | 40 | 80

30 | 10 | 30 | 30 | 10 | 70

Page 11 : LA RUE FROIDE
(The Cold Street)

Page 23 :

Page 31 : A SCALLOP MUST BE AT LEAST 4 INCHES TO BE CAUGHT.

Page 12 :

Page 22 :
Length **420 feet**
Width **35 feet**
Total weight **8,000 tons**
Maximum speed
22 m/h

Page 24 :

MEN'S ABBEY
WOMEN'S ABBEY

Page 29 : THEY'VE DONE SOME WORK HERE, HAVEN'T THEY?

Page 30 :

BRENT GOOSE
EEL
BLACK-HEADED GULL
COMMON SHELDUCK
GLASSWORT
CUTTLEFISH
SEA-BUCKTHORN
HARBOUR SEAL

Page 32 :

M	C	E	L	S	A	C	K	L
U	O	C	K	R	N	O		E
S	S	E	L	E	D	C	D	
L	O	Y	S	T	S	G	O	B
O	M	T	C	R	H	E	L	A
B	A	E	W	A	R	P	K	R
S	L	V	H	B	I	M	N	C
T	C	L	E	L	K	W	I	T
E	R	E	V	L	I	M	P	E

Page 36 :

Page 37 :

Page 38 : Number 2

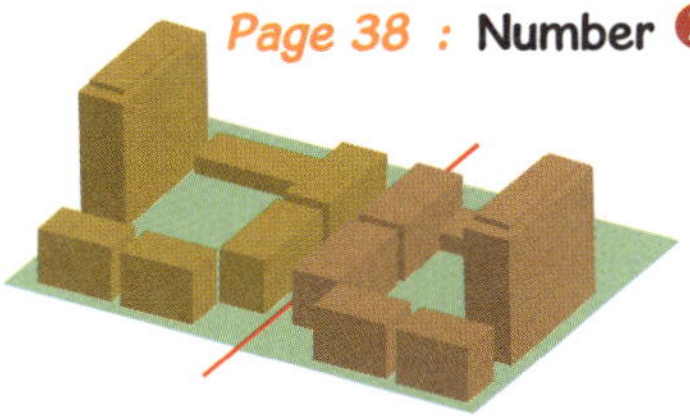

Page 41 : the **ALABASTER** coast

Page 41 :
These 2 mixtures are wrong.

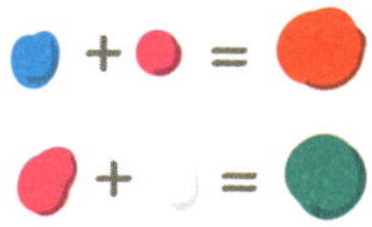

Page 42 : 

The Treasure belongs to the **KINGS OF FRANCE.**

Page 43 :
Bubble 3 is CORRECT!

Page 45 :

- SATURN > SATURDAY
- VENUS > FRIDAY
- APOLLO > SUNDAY
- DIANE (MOON) > MONDAY
- JUPITER > THURSDAY
- MERCURY > WEDNESDAY
- MARS > TUESDAY

Page 46 :

Page 50 :

Page 54:
Normandy cows have three different coats.
The **CURDLED** coat, the **BLOND** coat, and the **BRINDLE** coat

Page 47 : It is the **BUTTER** tower

Page 55 :

Page 52:
To equip everyone, we are missing:

- 1 life-jacket,
- 0 helmets,
- 2 paddles

Page 53:
The name of the mountain stream is:
THE ROUVRE

The human profile

Page 56 :

Page 57 :
The series of paintings by Monet is called **NYMPHÉAS.**

Page 58: Only two apple crates will be full. There will be 1 apple missing to fill the 3rd crate.

DISCOVER FRANCE IN A FUN WAY!

A collection of **PLAYFUL BOOKS** to encourage children to become acquainted with french culture.

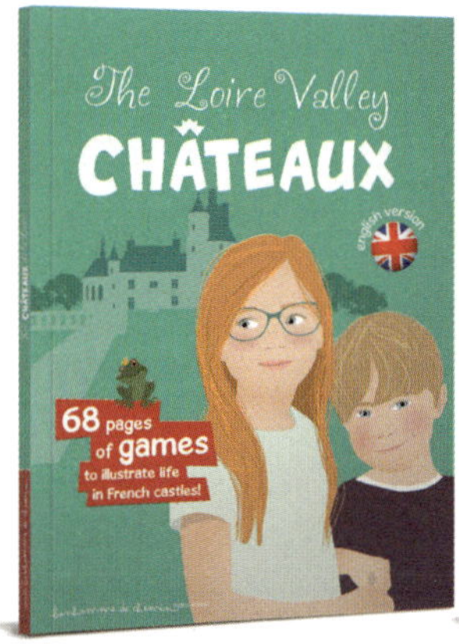

Authors: **Stéphanie and Hugues Bioret, Julie Godefroy**
Illustrators: **Julie Godefroy and Stéphanie Bioret**

Acknowledgements: ***Mrs Brigitte Lecourt****, Bayeux Museum, Guy Bioret and of course our favourite little proofreaders Camille, Martin and Angèle.*

Contact: tel. +33 (0)6 13 54 19 80
bonhommedechemin@orange.fr
www.bonhommedechemin.fr

In compliance with law no49956 from 16 July 1949 regarding publications for children
ISBN: 979-10-92714-33-3
Imprimerie Graphitilt (79)
Printed on PEFC paper
Printing completed in June 2019
Legal registration: June 2019

PEFC
10-32-3010
Certifié PEFC

Despite all the care put into the design and content of this book, it is still subject to change. Please feel free to send us your comments. Suggestions are also welcome.

IMPRIM'VERT®

Photo credits:

Hugues and Stephanie Bioret: *p.9: Caen castle walls; p.10: statue of William the Conqueror in Falaise; p.11: the Rue Froide in Caen; p.12: Bayeux tapestry, 11th century - special authorisation from the town of Bayeux; p.43: Le Bec-Hellouin*

Julie Godefroy: *pp.18-19: Arromanches; p.56: Carrouges castle; p.58: bowl of cider*

Honfleur Tourist Office: *p.51: the wooden steeple at Saint-Catherine's church*

CNES photo-library: *p.21: Chausey Island archipelago*

Pixabay: *p.2: Racine port; p.20: Granville by Mirek; p.29 Seagulls p.34: American cemetery in Colleville-sur-mer*

Creative commons: *p.2: goldfinch; p.11: Caen bombarded by Captain E.G. Malindine, N°5 Army Film & Photographic Unit-photographie B 6794 collection Imperial War Museums (collection no. 4700-29); p.14 : Garance (Rubia tinctorum) by Franz Eugen Köhler, Köhler's Medizinal-Pflanzen-List of Koehler Images; p.17: Royal Marine commando forces from the 3rd division moving inland from Sword Beach on the coast of Normandy, on 6 June 1944; p.24: engraving from Jumièges abbey by Louis Boudan-National Library of France; p.25 scriptorium; p.27: Saint Michael's spire by Thomas Dousseau; p.35: umbrella in Cherbourg from the website of the manufacturer* Le véritable Cherbourg; *p.38: Auguste Perret; p.49: anonymous star, Clint Eastwood by Metro Goldwyn Mayer; p.51 by Eugène Boudin*

© Adobe-Stock: *p.3: apple trees by © Gerhard1302; pp.4-5: Sainte-Marguerite-sur-Mer beach by © Suzanne Plumette; p.11: Quatrans house by © david-bgn; p.17: Omaha beach by © lindalim; p.20: rose watercolour by © lisima; p.21: dolphin by © lancesagar; p.24: Jumièges abbey by © lamio; p.25: dropped initial by Erica Guilane-Nachez; p.27: Mont-Saint-Michel abbey by © 4Max; p.29: Mont Saint-Michel abbey by © Elisabeth; p.30: salt marshes at Mont Saint-Michel by © Max Topchii, Eel (conger) by © Laure F, glasswort by © helenedevun; p.37: Etretat by © Sergii Mostovyi, tubes of paint by © stockphoto mania; p.34: Non-Violence sculpture by the artist Carl Reutersward by © CHG; villas in Houlgate by © Philippe Devanne; flat oysters by © Picture Partners; Jumièges abbey by © PackShot; p.35: horse-jump competition © Petra Eckerl; deep purple tulip in Moutiers forest by © JC DRAPIER; Cotentin, hike along the GR 223 path, Écalgrain bay by © aterrom; p.38: after-war architecture by © laguna35; p.39: Saint Joseph's church © arnaudmartinez; p.40: cliff in Etretat by © oscity; p.44: Rouen, old houses in the Old Market Square by © aterrom, Illustration by © Morphart, cog by © adimas, Gros Horloge by © aterrom; p.47: Rouen cathedral by © siempreverde22; p.48: Deauville Planks by © rh2010; p.50: Honfleur by © dvoevnore; p.52: The "Orne" river in Pont-d'Ouilly by © david-bgn; p.53: Natural site of the Rock of Oëtre by © david-bgn; p.54: Two dairy cows in a meadow in Normandy by © aquaphoto; p.57: Giverny gardens by © aterrom; p.58: apples by © Yvan Reitserof*